Cyclone

Cyclone

Robert Peake

Nine
Arches
Press

Cyclone
Robert Peake

ISBN: 978-1-911027-44-7

First published July 2018 by:

Nine Arches Press
Unit 14,
Sir Frank Whittle Business Centre,
Great Central Way, Rugby.
CV21 3XH
United Kingdom

www.ninearchespress.com

Printed in the United Kingdom by:
Imprint Digital

Nine Arches Press is supported using public funding by Arts Council England.

Supported using public funding by
**ARTS COUNCIL
ENGLAND**

for Valerie

and

remembering James

CONTENTS

"Lord, here comes the flood…"
Peter Gabriel

The Man with the Kindest Face

The rear-view glimpse is fleeting
as he lets you into the lane.

He might not have a face at all
or change it like a set of masks –

behind a newspaper in the waiting room,
sliding over to make room on the bus.

You resolve next time to look at him,
risk letting him look back at you.

You taste the salt in your throat,
and you hear him ask, *What's wrong?*

You smile at him and say, *Nothing.*
And you mean it. *Nothing at all.*

Nomansland Common

"These fragments I have shored against my ruins…"
– T.S. Eliot, *The Wasteland*

I.

                You wake up. Thursday.
In England, not that house, but the other
one, and you are married, and you are
employed, and today is a workday. It is
early. You flex the fingers of your dominant
hand. You are lying on it. You are lying on
your right-hand side, and the pillow is damp
around the right-hand corner of your mouth.
You roll out of bed onto your left leg.
The shock of it travels to the hip-socket,
left shoulder, the spine reverberates
in sympathy. You wake up. You are you.

Two egg cups greet the morning.
Tapping and slicing, you lay waste the shell,
meant to be broken from within, meant to be
the emergence of life from protective slumber,
the first waking, coated in the soil of blood –
a leaf periscopes, a small beak probes, shakes
off the dirt of its making, and you who have
forgotten, find it now underneath your nails
and curl it out with a dull knife, scrub it
out with a brush, mould the soft clay of your
belly over the first scar of your making.

II.

The taste of blackened sunlight,
the ash-taste of morning, stabbing the drapes.
We rise, assemble, tuck in, fall out, lie flatly
through our teeth about how much we love it here.

      Blackbird splashes
paint on the wall, a test of faith
its piezoelectric charm, and overtone,
the low hum of a foraging bear,
of diesel truck, trembling to stay still,
bright young man in the opioid clinic,
radial whirr of tyres losing their grip.

I am the spike at the top of the acorn,
splinter in smooth wood, punchline's sting.
That salty taste in the mouth, red spot
on your napkin, sliver of under-nail ice,
that's me –

      I am waiting, pincers aloft,
and abdomen throbbing, mandibles poised
on each side of my articulated face.
Step on me, on a crack, step up, fall in,
and be singed by the translucent barb
as it plunges through willing skin.

III.

How fast can you go
down the hill, your legs becoming springs,
becoming spring itself, arms winged out,
dodging the pollen-dander flak, you are
young, they say, and may it ever be so,
shuddering to a halt in the long gully,
a shadow passes over, dipping low –
how could you recognise your future
self without a name, a form, it is cold
for a moment in the dark before
thought, and the white grass trembles.

The new-born next door,
shielded from view, from the sun, blue eyes
in the process of taking colour, blue as water
before the ink curls in. Next door, the still
contentment of garden tasks. Next door, as if.
The other side of the fence. Just out of view.

IV.

A shadow passes over the meadow, effortless
in its cooling presence, a wake
of songbirds, for a moment stilled,
for a moment passed over
by a presence like night, a shoal of fish
beneath the barnacled hull,
tender in covering, blanket-soft,
the lids pulled over
our welling eyes, to shed a drop
in the pool of soft grasses,
which ripple, concentric,
in an unseen wind that blows
all things, together, onward, all things,
eventually into crossing,
into parting, into the covering-over
of life with – not death, exactly –
but the other side, the other life
in which cloud, meadow, fish, ship
reveal their true names to us –
flashes-through-sunlight, dark
moisture, ink of relentless progression.

A brush dipped
in clear water, the pigment's smoke,
a cipher of leaves in the swirled cup.
The hawthorn renounces her wedding vows.
Slow raptors finger the dryness of heat.
Nameless, in the new world, a congregation
of petals, root, trunk, and branches,
new leaves, in the unnamed world,
hold out their yellow hands to the rain.

A voice cries out
in a language you recognise, and the cloud –
for that is what it is, just a cloud –
retreats in spinal curvature over the hill,
which is grass, then soil, then stone,
a foetus in the centre, its open hand
a gesture of greeting, of saying "goodbye" –
and now you are on your knees, in a field,
jet-lagged, on a Wednesday, remembering
your name, a gift from your mother,
as the multiplication tables arrange
themselves before you, pieces for chess,
a calendar full of meetings in which
you can never say: for a moment, I was
that shadow, say, listen, I have been
to the other side of life, and a child
rests in the womb of the earth,
but instead stare down at your ink-stained
hands, and nod, and arrange your broken
face in a gesture of listening.

The man with the kindest face has change for a twenty

He doesn't look rich. Yet his pockets overflow with coins. "How much do you need?" he asks, and you tell him. You want to tell him more – that you need to believe, understand, be heard. He extends his closed hand like a magician. You expect nothing. You expect a dove to fly out from his sleeve. You open your hand, beneath his, and wait.

Village Panto

Now we come to the part where the smallest
children file onstage, in animal pyjamas,
the village hall pumping the dance number
they practiced since September, and still

don't really know, when the audience starts
clapping along to the music, because most
are related to one or another, a mum, gran,
uncle or aunt, and though they don't say

the L-word much, picking them up at school
or tucking them in at night, this is their
way of saying: yes the lights are blinding,
the jokes over even our heads, but we are

here in the dark, loving the way you miss
the cue, hands up when everyone's hands
are down, wanting to absorb like a black
sponge every drop of trepidation, so there

is only the thrill of being seen; clapping
to say: *give us everything, all you've got.*

Why I Should Be Over It By Now

(ten reasons for ten years)

Because it was a long time ago.

Because, after all, he was very small.

Because hawthorn blooms a lace cover for its thorns.

Because many couples don't have children (yet, ever).

Because you had choices (not choices).

Because beech-leaf orange rages the valley unchecked.

Because you look best in photos when you smile.

Overrated is making sense, because.

Because who can remember his name?

Because of the wonderful things he does.

Cognates of Grief

Kobus, Koos, Jago,
Jamma, Diegu, Joggi,
Ya'aqov, Yaakov, Iacobus,
Iacomus, Jakobus, Iakov,
Jakobe, Köbe, Iago,
Jaime, Diego, Santiago,
Yasha, Séamas, Siâms,
Yakobo, Jems, Jacques,
Jakku, Jaak, Jake,
Jack, Jim, Jimbo,
Jimmy, Jamie, Jay,
first, only, baby,
James.

Cyclone

I. Waterspout

My son, it has been ten years, and whenever
the wind sprays into my face, I taste the salt
of your absence. Hear me, above the engine roar
spinning your mother and me through the arc of space

from one place to another, on a globe gone flat
with the low drone of a world swept up in constant war,
and you, my child, are whisked darkly across the ocean
in the arms of its survivors, in a homemade raft,

alighting on pebbles you thought would be sand,
a mouth full of stones to reply to the uniformed guards
(I almost wrote – uninformed guards –) of the gates
of Jannah. It signals with a taste in the back of the throat,

that rises into a pillar of cloud to follow by day,
across the waters, troubled, and scattered with ash.

II. Steam devil

I see you in the exhalations of a steam train
wheezing through the local zoo, the whistle
whips my nephew's face around to face me,
alight with the joy of being startled, and safe.

The Tasmanian devil is far more solid,
except in cartoon form, spinning like a top.
At this age, I would spin free of my senses,
crashing into furniture, collapsing in a heap.

The brakes gasp, setting us down where we began,
stepping through the air to the hissing ground.
The wind is always spinning, all around us.
A puff of kettle steam confirms it. The devil's

greatest virtue is his patience, waiting
unseen, unheard, in the warm, moist air.

III. Tornado

Dorothy was no stranger to violence in the Midwest.
Her dog, who meant "everything", cleared "Indians"
from their ancestral lands, with a bark and a Federal
grant. They gave each a copper penny and a bowl of dust.

Her blood is in my blood. It boils in midnight sweats.
The parent of loneliness is sleep withheld. The damp
rises up from below the floor. The endless spiralling.
The broken pacts. Glass rattling in the basement.

Perfect girl in a field of poppies. Popping perfection pills.
We garland you with kisses, encircle the innocents,
as the scythe goes spinning on outside your window,
and the dark tilling begins in the green-sparked air.

First, I was a witch, then a twitch in the knowing tail.
The barometer is shaking, like an old woman's hands.

IV. Mesocyclone

Since the last place you'd dream of landing is here,
in the silt-choked afterlife of someone's grief,
we've become the vapour we feared would take us
down the rabbit hole these long dark years.

The sky is bright with promise, but we have fallen
into the trap of believing the lies of the sun – for
far too long we dreamt of falling, and never awoke.
Far too long, we dreamt of falling, and never awoke

into the trap of believing the lies of the sun, for
the sky is bright with promise, but we have fallen
down the rabbit hole these long dark years –
we've become the vapour we feared would take us

into the silt-choked afterlife of someone's grief,
since the last place you'd dream of landing is here.

V. Dust devil

Out of the bottle, and into the silted track, the abandoned
field, the rolling lanes of dune – you greet us just above
the wavering horizon, clawing marks into the fine beige sand.

Help the cracked and sun-washed ground profess its love,
reach up to the bleached sky with a spun-gold hand
your caffeinated gestures, a wild dance with much to prove –

let the bottled genius pelt us with sand, for how it glitters,
let the djinns contend with dervishes, lifting their hands
like birds, their skirts encircling a spark transmitter

between the gathering clouds and ionised land –
here is the lover's note that makes all wine seem bitter,
arcing encrypted messages across the golden sand.

Take us to the mountain, to worship at the feet of the sun
our mouths fill up with honey, our clothes have come unspun.

VI. Fire whirl

Come fractal, dog lick, crumpled gold foil, come respiration
of the embers, snowfall of ash on mountains and manicured lawns,
a corkscrew splits the line along the hills' ragged dentition

and we are smothered in the valley by a mud-red dawn,
smothered alive in our sofas by the news anchor's careful diction,
bleeping the word "napalm", bleeping the name of a son long gone,

into ash, into sea. Do not ask for more than this small cup,
be happy in your grief. Spin upright, little top, the fire's song
a full-grown fable meant to stir / whirr / whizz / cheer you up.

The Swedish candle chimes are pacing out their heat-praised gongs,
the vintage carousel, the blazing manes and tails, sweep low, rise up,
for a heart must be handled carefully, so as not to slip from the tongs.

Ablaze on a whizzing sphere, pricked with expired starlight,
with only a pillar of fire to follow through the vacuum of night.

End of the Meeting

"That's my eldest", says Blue Tie,
passing him around like bread.
We are smiling now, a sign
that the deal will close soon.

Two stone heavier, I look paternal –
eyes puffy with insomnia,
hair thinning like patience.
"Any pictures of your children?"

One photo, interred ten years in my wallet –
his eyes are also puffy, his hair is fluff.
He has not just scored a goal or graduated.
The death certificate read, "Occupation: infant."

Here I am, in my own occupation.

The man with the kindest face
in time of revolution

You see him in the uprising, subtle form amid the grandiose clatter, the bluster and blaster of the *plus ça* changing of the hide-bound old guard. He sweeps low like the willow, stealthy in the wind of crowds, skirting the margins of anger-bruised faces. He seems at home in this tempest. He seems happy.

The Opposite of Sleepwalking

I.

Summer insomnia, I dredge
the grasping hedgerows,
thorned tendrils reaching
to snag and slice me –
an opening in the cloud,
like two lips parting
interrupts the damp heat
that we call "close" –
as two bodies pressed
in the rot smell of grass,
a dusting of seed, chaff,
dander of straw, black dung
sat like immovable toads
daring me to cross their path.

II.

The edges fray between dream
and dream-dealer, card sharp
and simpleton taken for a ride.
I hide behind drowsing eyelids,
the electric sound of agitated
cloud, draw a blue spark from
the fur of the cat, arc toward
horizon, spreading my contrails
like a long line of genetic
disease, inherited malaise,
unrest in the populace, my shoes
untidy, my own self coming untied,
I hide behind wakeful catatonia,
and tremble with the thunder.

III.

The sky could be a bedsheet,
or a rear-projection screen
taking a little break right now
from machine-gunning still images
at our eyes to simulate movement.
I always wanted a ceiling painted
with clouds, stuck glow-in-the-dark
stars up there instead, the green
unnatural light so unlike perforations
in the black felt, revealing
a spotlit performance here on Earth,
curtains to twitch at the audience,
and me, left blinking on my mark
delivering a line I don't believe in.

IV.

A single oboe. The low wail that pervades
each morning's commute – milk steamer,
wheel rattle, thud of rubberised door.
A life is half lived without bass notes,
to bring the malady and concussion together –
or melody and precision – depending on the day,
while leaf-rot sticks to your worn-down shoes,
and the laces slap their mocking counter-rhythm.
What are cobbles for, but to trip on, in a drowned
rat's race to the bottom, wet dog's plea for change,
chugging down hot coffee and stale bagels,
hurrying to the next place you don't want to be –
and always the single oboe, the spitting reed,
crying for her lost calf in an field of hay.

V.

The green is going black, a loose rain,
the spots on the liver widening,
like pavement swallowed holy and whole –
here is the misbegotten toy soldier,
struggling between two concrete slabs,
propped on his plastic shoulder blades
over the pit of ordinary sidewalk ants.
Every day, I wake and walk suspended –
each cement square a probable trap door
into the familiar dark sludge
of self-decay. I tiptoe, ballerina-tight
from water cooler to cork message board,
pinned with slogans meant for another day.

VI.

The ground is permeable, as am I –
feather-soft in lamplight, packed
dust under desert sun, cracks
spreading electric, netting
pulled tight to the corpulent
thigh, mud-filled bladder,
meniscus, the slick of topsoil
fermenting to unction and froth,
as I step, and step sideways
grinding my heel for effect
over the microscope's corpses,
over the battlefield black
with the blood of unseen soldiers
in the mud, and the hardening clay.

VII.

Nothing is left but the wind,
which blows transparent
through my clothing,
what remains of my hair.
No village is safe
from other villages.
And yet we drink
from the same stream.
What becomes of longing
when the fire goes out?
Here are the cool embers
of the one I loved.
And so I walk through night.
And night walks with me.

The Mothra of Equanimity

After a night of not much sleep, I imagine my brain
a mound of spaghetti gelled together at the bottom
of last night's saucepan. Once again, I have failed
to live up to my picture of happiness, a ninja
slicing through his to-do list mindfully. Instead,
here I am slumped in my office chair, resting
on the sorest point in my back. The small pain
reminds me I am still awake, and that today is going
to be longer than other days. In fact, today hasn't
ever ended, but repeats in theme and variation,
sometimes the smell of honeysuckle, sometimes
its pendulant berries, but always today. I trapped
a moth with a glass cup and a postcard. He seemed
angry more than frightened, but I know it was just
program 271: escape at all costs – executing
in his Darwin-tuned neurology, so I lifted him
(or her) to an open window. The night was glowing.
The huge and beautiful eyes on his/her wings
looked back at me without a twitch of disapproval.
This morning is warm enough my teacup doesn't steam.
Trees' top leaves are sucking down glitzy sunlight
before the next rheostat swizzle of cloud.
A ninja steadies himself, glued to my ceiling,
waiting in cosmic silence to cover me with a cup.

Abduction

The spaceship landed, and we got in
leaving dinner to cool on the table,
nobody spoke, least of all them,
language stuck to the roof of our mouths,
tongues probing teeth for morsels.

Why should we tell unbelievers
(who would only call us "hayseeds" and "quacks")
how they glistened like soap on water,
how contact became more tender
the longer we let them wash over us?

Some say we grieve psychosis,
popped like sudsy bubbles before our eyes,
yet all of us felt it – that boundless,
fluid sense of a new life beginning
before we were set down in the field again.

It is their smell I miss the most –
resinous, both sweet and deep,
setting ions in the air on edge,
as though they were always evaporating,
half here, half returned to smoke.

I doubt they will ever come back,
sure we were chosen simply randomly,
the way a meteor chooses its crater –
still, on a clear night, in the arc of space,
I feel something pass over, call it grace.

The man with the kindest face pumps up your bicycle tyre

He keeps his eye on the task, fitting the hose and
squeezing the bulb, like a man-sized pollinator. The
tyre lets out a sigh of relief. "Good as new," he lies,
admiring your beat-up Schwinn. His eyes are trained
to see chrome, not rust, skip over the tar-blacked
chain. He glances up. He'd best be on his way.

Due Date
for TDR

Don't speak to me
                        of the darkness
            if you have not become
                                    the darkness
open your mouth
                        no sound
you open your mouth
                         again, no sound
close it because
                        there is no because,
in this marionette show
                        some call
the circus of life.
                        You scoop
    a drowning bug from the bath,
            but this
                    is not mercy,
you have become the weight
                        of the room,
and its contents
            have become
                        your contents,
and your breath
                has become
                        irretrievable,
and your flesh
        is stamped
in blue ink
                        just beneath
            the wrist
with the day
        of your departure.

Getting On With It

The weather forecast is a yellow frowny-face,
the radio static coalesces a rhythm,
the kettle, when poured, gives only steam.
With the snap of a switch, the walls change colour –
blink, and the trees defoliate; sneeze, and lose an ear;
ask how I ended up naked in this dumpster, and I'll
reply that things were just going that way.
Forget the slides, let's push each other on mood swings.
You be teeter, and I'll totter you up into space.
Forget the weather, let's mist-bathe and moon-bathe,
becoming more transparent with each exposure.
Let's film our lives and play the reel backwards.
Let's put on a happy song, and pretend to dance.
The economic forecast is a stick-man curled foetal.
I haven't stepped on a crack in twenty years.

To The Black Dog's Master

for Les Murray

O come, O come holy hellfire night
   where the table tops glow incandescent

And you return with a child's promise
   shaking a handful of dust in the wind.

You have copied my key and smashed the lock,
   invited yourself to my business meetings.

Dark saint, bright dagger, merciful inquisitor –
   not all questions have been answered.

Your flights unlisted, visits unannounced,
   trap door bulging just under the carpet.

Come rain of glass, breath of ice, fire
   in the blood of blood-shot eyes.

Please do go on ahead with your happy lives.
   I'll catch up. I'm just behind.

On the phone, a tic, and then it's your voice,
   at the keyboard, and click, your name.

Your phone lists all the ones we lost,
   but you can't let us see their number.

Company policy prohibits further contact.
   I can only confirm name, date, and occupation.

I can only confirm, yes, he was once your son.
  Sorry, I cannot disclose whether he loved you.

Let's just take five minutes for a breath of air.
  I'll be fine, Mr. Chairman, just tired.

I'll be fine, in my chair, in my bed, when you
  come, flashing scalpel, grinning teeth.

Mood Diary

I. Black Iris

How felt-like, this midnight,

purpled

to a bruise.

A fly in amber,

the black eye

searching

for escape.

Cry for me,

black dewdrop,

tracing the ruff

of your neck,

for I have lost

and in losing,

found only you

beside

the white curtains,

in a posture

of prayer,

a silhouette

to replace

the pane-fogged breath

a shadow

rising

in shadow.

Face me,

whoever you are,

staring me down

in the shaving mirror,

stroking black whiskers

from my Adam's apple,

swirling the refuse

with foam.
It is dark in the audience,

no light can enter
the ventricle.

Here, the matinee curtains,

here velvet,
crushed,
a frame
to enter
the emptiness
flickering
with the waltzes
of dust.
I come to you
on my knees,
wilting
as I have
always wilted
in your redolence.

II. Tar Pit

So begins the slow drip of another day.
So begins the deceptive patina of tar,
dusted in grit, tested with a single hoof,

clinging to the pads of your paw, stinking
of bone-char, black gum, automotive decay.
Coughed up like bits of lung on a beach
near La Brea, harder to tread than wet sand.

See how the bones pearl white for a necklace,
mastodon ribs suspended in long-dissolved sinews,
ghost threads of a once-forward motion.

Black gold pools the mouth of a protester, beaten,
black gold in the pupils, swapping ticker stocks.

Hit me says the baby in the racist folk tale,
and Br'er Rabbit can't resist putting in
his boot, sticking hated to hater in silent

embrace, for the child of tar says nothing,
but the greater the struggle, the closer
the two are held. Whither the poison flow?
Out from the gash of a sabred tooth, out

from the streets, asphalt melting in flames
whispered in riot shields and shopfront glass.
Has there ever been such a thing as progress?

Gum on our shoes, smoke on our hands. How can we
take, and take, even one step further?

III. Fulcrum

Which way are you going? asks hitchhiker to thumb.
Swinging low, sweet chariot – the arc of a babe in arms,
at the still point where gravity turns, neither toward
or away, facing the mendicant traveller, how many
on pin-heads, seated, are the angels looking over us,
how narrow the gap between this world and the next,
meniscus, bubble ready to give itself up in a pop.
But O! how it dances in the rainbow-splattered
colours of creation, swelling into roundness, thinning
the membrane between the air within and chill without.
Hush, little baby – a mockingbird, a diamond ring,
stoking the last of the embers with a minuscule gust,
as the suds go crackling, and the plug gets tugged,
(what else was a plug ever for, but pulling out?)
and down we go the motorway, our chariot made of fire.
What else was a plug ever for, but pulling out?
as the suds go crackling, and the plug gets tugged,
stoking the last of the embers with a minuscule gust –
hush, little baby – a mockingbird, a diamond ring,
the membrane between the air within and chill without,
colours of creation, swelling into roundness, thinning –
But O! how it dances in the rainbow-splattered
meniscus, bubble ready to give itself up in a pop,
how narrow the gap between this world and the next,
on pin-heads, seated, are the angels looking over us?
Or away, facing the mendicant traveller – how many
at the still point where gravity turns, neither toward,
swinging low, sweet chariot – the arc of a babe in arms –
Which way are you going? asks hitchhiker to thumb.

IV. Blind Lightning

Give Zeus my calling card. You call this a fucking storm?
Crack the glass globes of your overfed cheeks. I checked –

the forecast calls for vigilance, and sleep is overrated,
underserved, and deserving of the weak. I slurp my milk

with strychnine, all the better to see you my dear, wolfing
down the goodie basket and pounding my chest for more.

Second place is the first loser, so I'm told by my bumper sticker,
and whoever can't keep up is consumed in the fires of debt.

You made me! I screech, fleeing the scene, tearing my clothes,
but I will find a way to beat the forward march of time.

I will drink the absinthe, but who will wash the cup?
I moan while Rome is burning slowly down my throat.

Blow. Put your lips together. Even a bullet can whistle.

The man with the kindest face
runs for political office

He flip-flops like a mulberry leaf, over in the speckled wind, street performer on a forbidden spot, kite on an overstretched string, and you think at any moment: busted, you think of the headlines, and the tidal nature of popular appeal, Prometheus enduring his reward one liver-peck at a time.

Homesickness

Perched in the crotch of a tree,
contrails race toward intersection
drawing sutures across the sky
tightening our hold on the narrative
that the operation has been a success
the patient is recovering nicely
O exquisite corpse of my homeland,
fed upon by crows and financiers,
it was October, and the freezing rain
had not yet begun to decay you,
though your eyes were sunk deep
and your frail scissor limbs
grew inarticulate with pointing.
Whose fingers are left, unburnt?
Who is not wincing at the calendar,
huddled around a cackling fire,
counting the fuel in the woodpile?
How long will we breathe, mouth-on-mouth
into the blue lips of our forefathers,
the only family we have ever known?

Intermediate Sword Swallowing

After David Clarke

You know why the cashier behind the till
is saving up for chondrolaryngoplasty,
set to excise that final bite of apple
that Adam himself just couldn't get down.

The lips never get tired of blowing vodka
into a match, nor the teeth of tucking in
to the duvet, ball gag, or chewing gum.
The throat burns a different need.

Relax. You've come this far, and only a bit
more left to go. Who ever said living
life to the hilt was going to be easy?
Now extricate like an awkward party.

Your pinups are of throat muscles,
training them to be smooth and slack,
reassuring the touchy uvula, marked door
of a house passed over by the plague.

It's not that you won't keep making mistakes,
nick a tonsil, bruise the windpipe. Spit
blood into the sink, repeating your motto:
To scrape is human. To suppress, divine.

Stockholm

They came for me in time of peace.
They came clattering

over the cobbles, bright as bells,
in new uniforms.

They came in small brigades
of twos and threes,

hands on their hips, or pistols,
keeping their boots clean.

Bright angels, smartly dressed,
one looked like my son,

or how my son might have looked
if he survived.

Not one of their thirty fingernails
was dirty, escorting me

they all fell into marching
without orders.

I marched with them, into the alley.
Even in darkness they shone.

The tallest one knotted my blindfold
almost tenderly, I swear.

I could tell their hands were shaking
on their rifles.

Selfie Smile

The first act of aggression is to bare the teeth.
Then the backdrop swirls into view, in blues and greens.
Who wore this better? Now remember not to breathe,

or shift your chafing sandals, overstretch your jeans.
Smile through the pain, and call it pleasure, leisure,
declare yourself vacation's victor, holiday queen

keeping your friends at arm's length for good measure,
Machiavelli, now pull your phone in closer for a kiss,
the twist is not to show your own displeasure

with the weather, waiters, back-alley smell of piss,
but remember fans back home, in homely circumstances
fluorescent-lit, half-dying for a stroke of sunlit bliss

now capture what you came for, and give the lens a chance,
flash wide-eyed defiance, the loneliest romance.

Technological Advancements

Drones reach impossible places
so now the killing eye is always
with us, above us, whirring.

Thanks to hacks and leaks, we know
secrets that turn the stomach
from gold into lead.

The end of starvation is within reach
of a universal point-one-percent tax
on complaining to bus drivers.

Clear plastic safety covers
shield red buttons from toddlers
and presidents.

No home is complete without
gun safe, bomb shelter, fridge-freezer
all in one.

We give laser surgery to the hungry,
diamonds to pigeons, facelifts to cats.
We give because it hurts.

With Two

With two you will bomb a photo, request a table
for a romantic meal. The prints from two can convict.

Cross them for luck. First, live long and then, prosper.
With two you can ask "Where have the scissors gone?"

Use them to notch an arrow, curl fingertip crook
into a cradle, tighten the string and – quietly – let go.

It takes two to look good behind a cigarette, poke the eyes –
unless Moe makes a blade of his hand at the bridge of his nose.

Two for peace. Two for rudeness. Two for victory.
Two, inverted, walk their way right up my thigh.

Delusion, California

Welcome to town. You'll find it
all here: fire station, convenience,
butchery, find the people
willing to help, the sidewalks
unusually clean,
and the longer you stay,
the more it grows on you –
sunlight browning the grass,
sprinklers celebrating
an endless water supply,
housework done for minimum wage,
gas prices going down –
it will be this way from now
until the next now, having learned
to live in the moment
from your attractive yoga instructor,
learning to worry less
about things you can't control –
like those episodes, catching
your own eye in the mirror,
and wanting to salute, wanting
others to salute you, to make posters
where just one of your eyes
is as big as an ordinary man,
waking from a dream, and remembering
that you should always follow your dreams,
even when sometimes
people get hurt – remember omelettes,
acceptable losses, friendly fire,
remember greatness thrust upon you,
and thrust yourself out onto Main
Street to announce: I am here.
I have arrived. Citizens. Behold.

Free Will

"Breastmilk or bottle?" you don't get to decide
between the hard work of intimacy and plastic ease,
but weaning comes to us all and all too soon.

"Biscuit or cake?" the hallmark of childhood,
since sweetening the deal of your minor role makes it
easier to bounce between bullies and bicycle accidents.

"Tea or coffee?" the first question of adulthood,
since Lord knows you're going to need something
to get you through it all before retirement.

"Backgammon or bridge?" you must fill the time left
to you by your offspring, smile rememberingly
when they enter, and wave when they depart.

"Oak or Cedar?" you can decide if you like,
or if the whole business makes you squeamish, defer
to the next in line, and await further questioning.

Confirmation Bias

Beneath my skin, the red-white-and-blue
of muscle, tendon, artery – just enough
to satisfy Bastille Day, July the Fourth,
the waving last night of the Proms.

Livery goes back a brutal long way –
arms on the pub where we sip froth
making our livers ache, hands shake,
keeping us in our place at the bar.

Whence the revolution not of planets?
Around it comes again, freedom's thirst.
A ballot is as good as a bullet, hence
the psy-ops and cyber armies conscript.

Each of us, swayable as tall wheat.
Each of us full of barley and hope.
The stein of social media self-refilling,
as prophecies we make, then make come true.

Patient Refused Dental Anaesthesia

A threat to our way of life is a threat to our life.
The decision, therefore, was pre-emptive self-defence.

I was only protecting my country from what the internet
told me was going to happen, and look, so it did.

I watched the predictions come true, on nightly news,
while cleaning out the barrels of my mind.

True patriots, facing war, must discipline the body.
You must not let the molar facts dent in your mind.

Nothing about this struggle is going to be easy.
I'd rather drown in my own saliva than die on my knees.

The low-price leader heads the parade

as girls with plastic buckets flank him,
tossing free samples into the crowd:
Billy gets new ultra-slim comfort-fit
tampons, and Susan is the proud owner
of Gopher-Be-Gone Killz-Um Pest Poison.
The band behind isn't exactly marching,
but simultaneously playing tunes
for each demographic comprising today's
eager crowd: old-time for the old-timers,
electronica for the tween overtones,
nursery rhymes for the little ones,
clinically proven to lull children
and pets into a sense of security. Speaking
of which, here comes the homeland team
and don't they look great in sponsored
apparel – the brand-name ones to beat.
Well, send in the clowns, in their tiny
clown-car, so fuel efficient it's hilarious.
Now here comes this year's pageant queen,
and Bob, do I have this right, the voting
happened a little differently this year?
That's right, Chuck, instead of one person,
this year our dear townspeople elected
individual body parts from different girls,
which have been reassembled atop this float,
and just look at that wave, that smile –
two of our most popular items this season.

"Confident Middle-Aged Man Sitting and Smiling Against White Background"
(after the stock photo)

The way small motes flickered in sun, the way disaster
seemed to be around every corner, but never came.

Go on, snap my picture. I'll serve for a wax seal,
de-barb-ing, un-stinger-ing, making at once milquetoast

and reputable whatever it is you're trying to sell.
I put the harm in harmless, the pain in counterpane,

I come from a long line of, "He seemed like such a nice guy"
when they bust the attic padlock and smell corpses.

I'm the one you least expect, an owner of neckties,
poster child for the social contract, signed in faeces.

The way dust was never more than dust, but we were led
by brilliant slogans and hefty jingles to believe.

The way our mothers used to whisper, "You'll be great."
The way the handle of a handgun was made for my-sized hand.

Inventions

A bicycle fitted with a smog generator
to be treated as an equal with cars.

A ballot written in invisible ink.
A tree whose leaves double as tinfoil.

A newspaper that changes its story
based on your political views.

A gun scope that finds, downloads
and displays baby photos of its target.

Breakaway seat belts for messy divorces.
Bulletproof backpacks for schoolchildren.

A stick to keep your phone at arm's length.
Bullets coated in anaesthetic.

The man with the kindest face helps you rearrange your wardrobe

It's not his thing. But he holds out an arm for you to drape with coats and hook with hangers. Where does all this stuff come from? He smiles. You excavate the sarcophagus, victim of your own fashion sense. Here is the sleeve where you wiped your nose in the wind. Here is the lipstick-pocked collar you would rather forget. Too plump now for this, too skinny for that. Do you think I could still pull this off? you turn to ask. Only a curtain replies, shrugging in the breeze.

What Will Survive Us

Bronze statues of men on horses.
Small pieces of tarmac, glittering like shells.
Skeletal towers, disconnected.
Concrete hives with glassless windows.
Yellow foam congregating in eddies.
White bridges overtaken by gulls.

Magpie

half-ghost, half-demon,
standout in all weathers
rowing your rudder of tail.
If only things were so. If only
the dark in me was feathered,
divided, quill-by-quill from light,
as in the first piebald making
of the dung-world I carry rolled,
collecting hay and human dust.
O sucker for the glitzy thing.
O mixed-up bird, mirroring.
What do you see in tinsel-gleam?
How long have you waited
to flash through these branches,
half-shadow, half holy glow?

Waking Up to the Last Winter on Earth

The last of the junipers have pummelled the ground.
   The dark ground, the rotting ground.

No mystery to the guttered eaves singing.
   The old songs, the rain songs.

Here come planets, a speck of dust in the eye.
   The sharp pain, the dull pain.

Nothing left for it but two white pills.
   The remedy, the cause.

A burnt switch of reed is waving us on.
   The last goodbye, the first goodbye.

The spokes of the bicycle become invisible.
   Their one trick, their best trick.

The dead struggle to get comfortable.
   The shifting, and shifting.

We have become what our ancestors feared.
   The power, the curse.

Letter to the Last Megafauna

My friends, you wouldn't like it here, moss
squelching underfoot, lean drizzle
tickling your rivulets, bare trees.

We'd give you names like Babar, Dumbo, Topsy,
then shackle your legs for safety (ours),
parade you in a car for entertainment (ours).

Everywhere we go (archaeology shows) the giants
disappear – save you, the last of the mammoths,
eyelid creased with wrinkles, black eye watching.

Some say we compare our manhood to your tusks,
and feel ashamed. I say your remind us of more –
raising clouds like smoke on columnar feet.

First we trained you to the chain, now rope,
soon a string will keep you in place.
It has come to this: elephant or skyscraper.

My friends, stay put, stay huge, stay bulldozer slow,
uprooting acacia and spurting fountains of mud
at the barrels of cameras and rifle scopes alike.

I write to you from the damp sponge of England,
but red dust swills my nostrils, and sun drums my hide.
I could stand upright in the chambers of your heart.

Insults for Trees

Knot-navel, sour puss, gurning apopxlect –
your petals go to ground, firing for effect
wort-weeper, sap seeper, bark bite specked,
weft gone warped, and cross-grain wrecked.

Root-router, carbon-doubter, groundwater pump,
sucking up toxins like a living waste dump,
squirrel-coddler, mammal-fodder, spineless chump,
bird's nest protector with a single branch thump.

Wood-giver, wind-cheater, thorny eye sore,
felled for the asking when the neighbours get bored,
air-cleanser, soul-mender, draft-dodger of the war
you make a lousy window, you make a better door.

Collective

Adam named the beasts,
but the tribes of wildflower
name themselves.

An omen of buttercups,
a banishment of dandelions,
kaleidoscope of fern.

Who we are, who we
are not – edged in black earth
and mist-white air.

A papacy of silver birch,
a memory-lapse of meadow grass,
a concubine of ivy.

You say "Grove of beeches."
They say, "Still below,
ablaze above."

Reading Dostoevsky in the John Lewis Café Welwyn Garden City

The family before me has left a mess,
and so has Dimitry Fyodorovich –
shortbread crumbs ground into carpet;
blood stiffening his handkerchief.

The service is prompt and attentive
when you flash a hundred-rouble note,
or signal yourself as among the gentry
with a blazer and a public-school smirk.

The revolution has not yet come.
The existence of God remains debatable.
Young Fabians pamper their underdogs.
Teacups clink in fair-priced saucers.

A holy fool, a duel with pistols,
and Gemmas, Gemmas everywhere.
In the fitting rooms, the requirement
to give a strong but considered opinion.

Yes, yes, I am all finished here.
Yes, yes, it was all quite nice.
It is only that I am dying, dear brother –
can't you tell by my untouched Assam?

Berry-Coloured Scarf

The day began, almost biblical –
Moses parting frizz-frazzled hair,
Noah in floods of tears by the phone,
Jonah swallowed by his parents' divorce.

Low clouds bumped into each other
like newbies at the roller rink,
a kiss from summer blew on the breeze,
trees brown and orange as the '70s.

I was popular with the squirrels,
and that was all that mattered –
berries red as teenage lipstick,
mud and moss farting under foot.

Walk with me to school. I'll carry
your burdens, crack immature jokes.
Hair soft and fawn as corduroy,
cheek spots flushed with cold.

Failure to Thrive

I awoke, late afternoon, to a summer storm,
realising I had done none of the things
that the dead white men, who wrote history,
expected me to do to get added to their book,
and that the stream of productivity, running on
like an endless sentence from the past, was one
I punctuated far too often with a nap. The smell
of the rain came through the smallest window crack.
It was late summer. The rain had no idea of its
ending, and the smell was great with promise
for a week of gentle breezes pushing sculptures
of white cloud, the kind I could never write about
well enough to distinguish myself from the 773,000
cloud poems Google offers up to me for a click,
in point three eight seconds, because that's how fast
you have to be now to be somebody. The spare room
I favour sleeping in by day became almost imperceptibly
green, in the shadow of a thunderhead's contemplation,
yet I was there to see it, with the cat, who said nothing.

The man with the kindest face checks your passport

He glances up, then back at your picture, like a game of peek-a-boo. Leafing through the stamps, he seems pleased with your decisions. He presses down his own approval, pulls up quickly not to smudge. Doesn't he ever get bored? He flips the booklet shut like a card trick, levers it back, bowing at the wrist. You take it with both hands, to be sure.

Horse Optimism

Rain sweetens the grass,
and the sun makes it tall;
no flies on windswept days;
no restless leaves when calm.

At a distance, I see where you are.
Up close, I smell where you've been.

Sun dries the mud,
dew decorates the field.
Lie down in summer heat,
stamp against the chill.

Halfway through every journey out
we begin the ride back home.

Sweet grass from rainy days
a field sparked with dew
breeze to blow the flies away
the sight, then smell of you.

Acknowledgements and Thanks

Gratitude to the publications in which some version of these poems first appeared:

'Nomansland Common' (I-III) in *Under the Radar*; 'Delusion, California' in *December Magazine*; 'Free Will' on *Queen Mob's Teahouse* (queenmobs.com); 'Patient Refused Dental Anaesthaesia' in *Domestic Cherry*; "'Confident Middle-Aged Man Sitting and Smiling Against White Background"' in *The North*; 'Getting on With It' in *Poetry Salzburg Review*; 'The Low-Price Leader Heads the Parade' in *Woven Tale Press Magazine*; 'What Will Survive Us' on *Sustainable St. Albans* (sustainablestalbans.org); 'Letter to the Last Megafauna' in *A Poetry of Elephants* (ValMor Press, 2016); 'Collective' on The Clearing (www.littletoller.co.uk/the-clearing/) 'With Two' in *The Long-Islander*; 'Homesickness' on *Rattle Poets Respond* website (www.rattle.com); 'Reading Dostoevsky in the John Lewis Café Welwyn Garden City' on PoetryBay (www.poetrybay.com); 'Inventions' in *The Interpreter's House*; 'Selfie Smile' was published in *Poetry Salzburg Review*.

Thanks in particular to Jane Commane for her superb editorial insight, to Isabel Galleymore and Paul Stephenson for their comments on earlier drafts of these poems, and to my family for their enduring support.